# The Ghost Tree

Written by Jean Holkner
Illustrated by Caroline Campbell

The tree in front of my bedroom window
is turning to gold.

The wind blows the leaves to the ground
and soon they're wrinkled and brown.

I watch my dad raking them over the garden
and I'm sad. Winter is nearly here.

In the morning, I get out of bed
and pull up the blind.
It's still dark outside,
and there's even a star in the sky.

My tree looks cold and bare,
and the twigs are like little dry sticks.
I cough, and go back to bed.

Dad brings me steaming hot porridge
with lots of raisins in it.
But I'm not hungry.
I snuggle back under my blankets
and close my eyes.

The wind shakes the tree,
making it go "tap, tap, tap"
against the window.

I dream that I'm lost in snow.
The world is all white—even the sky.

It’s very cold, and I think
my feet have gone away somewhere.
Instead of hands, I have two ice-blocks
inside my gloves.

Then I see the tree.
It is covered in snow and stands like a ghost,
its arms up high, its thin stick fingers
pointing up into the frozen air.

Then it starts to come towards me.
I try to run, but I have no feet,
and I'm nearly buried in the deep snow.

The ghost tree is coming closer . . . closer . . .

H E L P !!!

Suddenly, I'm back in bed.
My blankets are lying on the floor.
No wonder I'm cold!

Dad covers me up again.
The tree is an ordinary tree again.

My cough is better.
Around the trunk of my tree,
a circle of yellow daffodils
has sprung out of the earth.
I pick one and put it in a glass
on the window-sill.
A bird comes to look.

Today, my tree is covered in pink blossoms.
It doesn't look at all like a ghost—
more like a ballet dancer.
I draw a picture of it with my crayons.

The sun is warm on my back.
The blossoms have blown away,
but I think some kind of fruit is coming.
Summer must be on the way.